"THE KOREAN KITCHEN:
A VISUAL FEAST OF 100
AUTHENTIC FLAVORS"

100 SERIES PART1 IN KOREA

Richard Hong : A Distinguished Leader Balancing Family, Career, and Care

In the bustling heart of South Korea, Richard Hong stands as a testament to the delicate art of balancing familial responsibilities, a thriving career, and the noble duty of caring for his grandmother. Currently serving as the Director of Telecommunications in the nation, Richard's journey in Korea is not only marked by professional accomplishments but also by a deep commitment to family.

Amidst the dynamic landscape of the telecommunications sector, Richard has spent dedicated years as a Telecommunications Director, contributing significantly to the technological advancements that characterize Korea's communication infrastructure. His expertise in the field has not only shaped the nation's connectivity but has also allowed him to create a stable and nurturing environment for his own family.

At home, Richard is not just a telecommunications professional but a devoted father to his son and daughter. Beyond the demanding corporate world, he embraces the joys and challenges of parenthood, instilling values and creating lasting memories for his children. Simultaneously, he takes on the role of a compassionate caregiver for his grandmother, embodying the Korean tradition of filial piety.

Richard Hong's narrative is one of resilience, passion, and a harmonious blend of professional success and familial warmth. Whether navigating the intricacies of telecommunications or cherishing moments with his loved ones, Richard stands as a beacon of inspiration, proving that a meaningful life is one that embraces both professional achievement and the profound connections of family.

Hotteok, a sweet Korean embrace, weaves a magical spell with its golden, crispy exterior and a gooey, indulgent center. Each bite is a symphony of warmth and sweetness, an ode to the cozy delights of Korean street food. The caramelized sugar and nutty filling create a dance of flavors that transcends the ordinary pancake. Hotteok isn't just a treat; it's a nostalgic journey through the bustling streets of Korea, capturing the essence of comfort and joy in every delectable bite. It's a dessert that whispers tales of tradition and modern-day delight in perfect harmony.

"THE KOREAN KITCHEN:

A VISUAL FEAST OF 100

AUTHENTIC FLAVORS"

100 SERIES PART1 IN KOREA

Written by Richard Hong

Tables

••

Tables

●●

Tables

Prologue

Embark on a culinary odyssey through the heart of Korea with "The Korean Kitchen: A Visual Feast of 100 Authentic Flavors" This visually stunning book is a celebration of the rich and diverse world of Korean cuisine, capturing the essence of 100 iconic dishes that define the Korean culinary landscape.

From the comforting warmth of Kimchi Jjigae to the savory delights of Bulgogi, each dish is a symphony of flavors that reflects the vibrant cultural tapestry of Korea. Imagine the sizzle of Grilled Pork Belly (Samgyeopsal), the spice of Tteokbokki's Rice Cake Stew, and the soothing comfort of Sundubu Jjigae's Soft Tofu Stew. "Korean Culinary Tapestry" doesn't just showcase recipes; it tells the stories behind each dish, providing a deeper understanding of the cultural and historical significance that makes Korean food so special.

Dive into the pages to explore the artistry behind Seafood Pancake (Haemul Pajeon) and the bold flavors of Spicy Stir-fried Baby Octopus (Jjukkumi Bokkeum). Experience the umami explosion of Fermented Soybean Paste Stew (Doenjang Jjigae) and the delightful sweetness of Hotteok, a traditional Korean pancake.

The book not only tantalizes your taste buds but also visually enchants with captivating images of each dish. Each turn of the page is an invitation to savor the beauty and diversity of Korean culinary culture.

"The Korean Kitchen: A Visual Feast of 100 Authentic Flavors" is not just a cookbook; it's a cultural exploration, an invitation to embrace the spirit of Korea through its extraordinary cuisine. Whether you're a seasoned food enthusiast or a curious newcomer, this book promises a journey of discovery into the heart and soul of Korean culinary heritage. Immerse yourself in the stories, flavors, and traditions that make these 100 dishes a testament to Korea's rich gastronomic tapestry. Get ready to embark on a culinary adventure that will leave you inspired, hungry, and with a newfound appreciation for the wonders of Korean food.

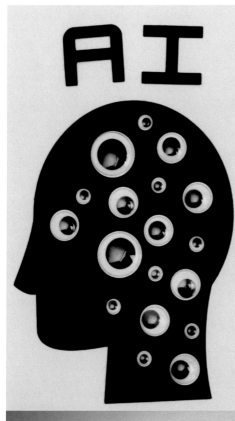

AI

Korean traditional cuisine is a symphony of flavors that dances on the palate, embodying centuries of culinary artistry and cultural richness. From the soul-warming embrace of Kimchi Jjigae to the tantalizing sizzle of Bulgogi on the grill, each dish is a celebration of tradition and a testament to the deep-rooted respect for nature's bounty.

In the heart of Korean culinary heritage lies the art of balance — a delicate equilibrium of sweet, savory, spicy, and umami. Bibimbap, a vibrant medley of colors and textures, invites you to create your own masterpiece, while the intricate layers of Japchae weave a tapestry of glass noodles, vegetables, and savory beef.

The table becomes a canvas, adorned with an array of banchan, those small yet impactful side dishes that transform a meal into a communal experience. Each bite tells a story of meticulous preparation, from the meticulous fermentation of Kimchi to the slow braising of Galbijjim, where succulent short ribs soak up the essence of soy and sweetness.

As you indulge in the crispiness of Hotteok or the chewy satisfaction of Tteok, you embark on a sensory journey through time. Korean cuisine isn't just about sustenance; it's a cultural narrative, a way of connecting with the past while embracing the present.

From the bustling street markets offering Odolbokkeum's spicy pork backbone to the serene elegance of Hanjeongsik's meticulously curated feast, Korean traditional food is an exploration of contrasts and a celebration of harmony. Each dish reflects the seasons, the landscape, and the profound respect for nature ingrained in Korean philosophy.

So, whether you're enjoying the communal ritual of Korean barbecue or relishing the simplicity of a bowl of Doenjang Guk, remember that Korean cuisine is more than a meal – it's a profound expression of identity, a journey through time-honored flavors that continue to captivate and inspire.

1. 된장찌개 (Doenjang Jjigae)
: Fermented Soybean Paste Stew

Let's take a moment to appreciate Doenjang Jjigae, a Korean dish that offers unparalleled comfort and satisfaction comparable to a warm embrace. This delectable delicacy is a harmonious blend of fermented soybean paste, vegetables, and tofu, providing an unforgettable umami experience. The aroma is a delightful combination of savory and earthy notes, evoking nostalgia and reminding us to cherish every moment. So, indulge your senses and immerse yourself in tradition by savoring every bite with a spoon. This dish is a testament to the notion that life's simplest pleasures, rooted in heritage and tradition, often provide the most profound satisfaction, transcending time and culture.

2. 김치찌개 (Kimchi Jjigae)
: Spicy Kimchi Stew

Indulge in a flavor-packed meal with Kimchi Jjigae, the ultimate Spicy Kimchi Stew! With every spoonful, experience a burst of flavors as the fermented kimchi, succulent pork, and smooth tofu come together in a fiery explosion. This stew is not just a dish but an immersive experience through traditional Korean cuisine, providing comfort and satisfaction in every bite. A celebration of humble ingredients that are transformed into a delectable masterpiece, it's a culinary journey that beckons you to embrace the Korean spirit. So grab your chopsticks and savor the rich blend of culture and taste that Kimchi Jjigae has to offer.

3. 떡볶이 (Tteokbokki)
: Spicy Rice Cake Stew

Immerse yourself in the vibrant streets of Korea and experience the unforgettable Tteokbokki. This dish is a sensory explosion, featuring chewy rice cakes soaked in a sweet and spicy sauce that will leave you feeling euphoric. The rich red sauce coats each piece, bursting with flavors that transport you to lively markets and bustling gatherings. Tteokbokki is more than just a dish; it captures the essence of street-side delicacies. Its perfect chewiness, combined with a bold and rich sauce, creates a party in your mouth, celebrating all things hearty, daring, and straightforward. Every bite is a culinary masterpiece, a love letter to your taste buds.

4. 잡채 (Japchae)
: Stir-fried Glass Noodles with Vegetables

Indulge in the captivating Japchae, a culinary masterpiece that tantalizes the palate with its harmonious blend of flavors. The sweet potato noodles, with their satisfying chew, pair impeccably with an array of vibrant vegetables, culminating in a delightful feast for the senses. The addition of succulent beef only enhances the savory-sweet fusion, resulting in a truly euphoric dining experience. Japchae is more than just a meal; it's a symbol of Korean cuisine's artistry, leaving an indelible impression on every food lover. So, let us raise our chopsticks and salute this remarkable dish to the gastronomic gods!

5. 김치전 (Kimchi Jeon)
: Kimchi Pancake

Kimchi Jeon is the ultimate Korean pancake that embodies all things crispy and delicious. With its golden-brown exterior, it's hard not to be drawn in by its savory aroma. However, it's the chewy texture and delicious kimchi-infused flavor that makes it truly irresistible. Every bite is a sensory delight that will transport you straight to Korea. The dish is crafted with love and care, and the result is a pancake that will make you want to dance with happiness.

6. 갈비찜 (Galbijjim)
: Braised Short Ribs

Listen up, foodies! There's a Korean delicacy that reigns supreme in the realm of gastronomy – Galbijjim! This dish is a flavor explosion that will teleport your taste buds to another dimension. Imagine juicy, tender short ribs slow-cooked in a soy-based sauce that'll make your toes curl. It's like a sweet and savory dance party in your mouth that will take you on a journey through Korean heritage. Trust us, this is not your average meal; it's a culinary masterpiece, a work of art crafted with passion and skill. The sauce, the texture, and the savory goodness make it an unforgettable experience that celebrates the best of Korean traditions. So, grab a fork and enjoy the ride!

7. 비빔밥 (Bibimbap)
: Mixed Rice Bowl with Vegetables and Gochujang

Prepare to have your taste buds blown away by the majestic dish that is bibimbap! This Korean sensation is a mouth-watering symphony of colors and flavors that will have you begging for more. Each spoonful is a tantalizing combination of juicy meats, fresh veggies, and a fiery kick from the gochujang sauce. The crispy rice crust adds a satisfying crunch to every bite, and the dish as a whole is a masterpiece that celebrates the beauty of diversity. Bibimbap is not just a meal, it's a work of art that proves the power of simplicity. With its fresh ingredients and bold flavors, this dish is a must-try for any culinary adventurer!

8. 쌈장 (Ssamjang)
: Thick Spicy Paste for Wraps

Introducing the superstar of Korean cuisine: Ssamjang, the saucy enchantress who brings magic to every meal! This fiery potion blends tangy fermented soybean with gochujang spice to create a symphony of mouth-watering flavor. One taste and you're hooked, as the bold umami and spicy kick take your taste buds on a ride they won't forget. Ssamjang isn't just a condiment, it's a way of life! Pair it with smoky grilled meats and fresh greens for a taste sensation that'll light up your senses. So, take a journey of taste with Ssamjang at the helm and discover the culinary wonderland that is Korean cuisine. Get ready to be spellbound!

9. 감자탕 (Gamjatang)
: Pork Bone Soup with Potatoes

Are you ready to experience the cozy, soul-warming embrace of the Gamjatang? This Korean wonder-soup is a work of art that tantalizes your tastebuds with tender pork, a blend of spices, and velvety potatoes. Every sip of the broth takes you on a journey through the heart of Korean flavor, with each spoonful bringing a feeling of pure satisfaction. The Gamjatang is more than just a soup; it's a warm hug from the inside, a dish that will fill your heart and belly with pure joy!

10: 양념치킨 (Yangnyeom Chicken)
: Seasoned Fried Chicken

Move over plain old fried chicken, Yangnyeom Chicken is the new sheriff in town, and boy oh boy, does it pack a punch! With a golden, crispy exterior and tender, juicy meat, it's like biting into a flavor explosion! The sweet and spicy yangnyeom sauce is where the magic happens. It's like a sticky hug for your taste buds, leaving a finger-licking aftertaste that you won't forget. This is not your average fried chicken; it's a heavenly symphony of texture, flavor, and culture that will make your heart sing. Get ready to indulge in a crispy, zesty slice of Korean heaven!

If you add squid, mussels, etc. to Kimchi pancake, you can feel the flavor even more. It is still an indispensable taste for Koreans.

11. 계란찜 (Gyeran Jjim)
: Steamed Egg Casserole

Let's take a moment to appreciate the Korean superstar dish, Gyeran Jjim! It's the ultimate hug in a bowl, with a velvety texture and a delicate egg flavor that will make you weak in the knees. Every spoonful is a journey through a symphony of flavors, reminding us of the beauty of simplicity. This dish is a culinary masterpiece, a poem written in eggs, that will leave you feeling warm and fuzzy inside. So let's give a round of applause to Gyeran Jjim, the timeless classic that reminds us why we love Korean cuisine so much!

12. 김밥 (Kimbap) – Korean
: Seaweed Rice Rolls

Kimbap, the artful Korean seaweed rice rolls, is a portable feast that encapsulates the essence of Korean ingenuity. Each bite unveils a harmonious blend of seasoned rice, fresh vegetables, and savory proteins, tightly wrapped in seaweed. Its simplicity belies the explosion of flavors that dance on the palate, a culinary symphony that transcends the boundaries of a humble roll. Kimbap isn't just a snack; it's a cultural journey, a celebration of balance, and a testament to the delightful creativity embedded in Korean culinary traditions. Each roll is a savory adventure, a bite-sized masterpiece.

13. 육회 (Yukhoe)
: Korean Beef Tartare

Synonymous with Korean cuisine, yukhoe is a dance of textures and flavors that elevates beef to an exquisite art form. Velvety tender beef adorned with the flavor of sesame oil and the richness of pear creates a symphony of flavors. Each bite is fresh and refined, proving that harmony can be found in simplicity. Yukhoe is a journey of the senses beyond the concept of yukhoe, an invitation to experience the sublimity of marinated meat, and a food that reveals the depth of Korean gastronomy.

14. 장어구이 (Jangeo Gui)
Broiled eel

Hold onto your taste buds, folks! Jangeo Gui, the king of grilled eel, is a flavor-packed journey that'll teleport you to culinary paradise! The eel's juicy tenderness, infused with a flavor-fiesta, gets jiggy on the grill, giving off a seductive smoky-sweet aroma that is hard to resist. Every morsel is a mouth-watering tribute to the ocean's treasures, grilled to perfection, and dripping with a rich caramelized glaze that bursts with an explosion of umami. It's clear that Korean cooking's artistry is on full display here, with the delicate flakiness of the eel adding finesse to this culinary masterpiece. So, go ahead, embrace the sea's gifts, and let Jangeo Gui take you on a tantalizing taste adventure!

15. 삼겹살 (Samgyeopsal) : Grilled Pork Belly

A sensory masterpiece awaits in the realm of Samgyeopsal; a tribute to both porcine ethereal pleasures, encapsulating the very essence of Korean hospitality. The pork belly slice a work of art, is seared to perfection over open flames, a balance of crisp and succulent that beckons the senses. The ritual of the table, where each guest is invited to take part in the art of grilling, transforms the meal into a celebration of community and shared delight. The aroma of smoke and spice intertwine, weaving a symphony of flavor that dances upon the tongue, beckoning one to savor each delectable bite. Samgyeopsal is more than a dish; it's a journey of the senses, an ode to the bonds of friendship, and a celebration of the exquisite joy found in every melt-in-your-mouth morsel.

16. 불고기 (Bulgogi)
: Sweet and Savory Grilled Beef

A mystical dish that transcends taste, Bulgogi is a symphony of flavors that dances on the tongue. Each succulent slice of grilled beef, infused with a magical blend of soy sauce, sugar, and spices, is a tribute to the art of Korean cuisine. The sweet and savory marinade, infused with a hint of caramelized perfection, invites the senses on a magical journey, weaving a tale of tradition, innovation, and pure culinary bliss. Bulgogi is not just a dish, but a celebration of the mysteries of flavor, a chance to savor the rich, enchanting tapestry of Korean cuisine, and a reminder of the joy found in every mouthwatering bite.

고등어 구이 (Godeungeo Gui)
Grilled Mackerel

Behold the grilled mackerel known as Godeungeo Gui, a tantalizing seafood creation. As you take a bite, the smoky notes and succulent mackerel flesh imbue it with a savory melody of smoke and tenderness. With every bite, the ocean's essence bursts forth, harmonizing with the crispness of the skin. The symphony of flavors and aromas captures the sea's spirit, inviting you to partake in the oceanic bounty. With each succulent bite, Godeungeo Gui is a love letter to the seaside, an invitation to savor the ocean's embrace in every delectable morsel.

18. 냉면 (Naengmyeon)
: Cold Buckwheat Noodles

Behold, the oasis of Naengmyeon, a dish that beckons as a balm for the sweltering heat. The strands of buckwheat noodles, taut and supple, cradle a cascade of flavors, each a brushstroke on the canvas of the palate. The broth, born of icy splendor, carries a symphony of notes from the tang of vinegar to the richness of beef. Adorned with a crown of verdant vegetables, and garnished with the merest hint of mustard, Naengmyeon is a journey of rejuvenation, a tribute to the harmony of texture and contrast. A Korean delicacy crafted with skill and finesse, it transforms a meal into a refreshing escape, a celebration of cool satisfaction.

19. 순두부찌개 (Sundubu Jjigae) :
Soft Tofu Stew

Sundubu Jjigae, the exquisite Soft Tofu Stew, is a tantalizing blend of comfort and complexity.
This divine dish, with its lush tofu adrift in a fiery ocean of flavors, envelops the spirit in
warmth. With each spoonful, a symphony of textures unfolds, from the silken tofu to the
kaleidoscope of vegetables and the rich broth. This bubbling cauldron is more than a mere
meal; it is a celebration of Korean home cooking, a tribute to the heart and soul of the nation's
cuisine. Sundubu Jjigae is a culinary hug, a melody of spice and tenderness that echoes
through time, making it a beloved staple among Korean delicacies.

20. 옥수수 찜 (Oksusu Jjim)
: Steamed Corn

Oksusu Jjim, the humble yet delightful Steamed Corn, is a celebration of simplicity and natural sweetness. Each golden kernel, infused with a gentle steam, bursts with a cornucopia of flavors. The tender texture and the inherent sweetness evoke a nostalgic connection to the fields. Oksusu Jjim is more than a dish; it's a journey to the heartland, a reminder of the sun-kissed fields and the pure joy found in the uncomplicated beauty of corn. This Korean favorite stands as a testament to the art of appreciating nature's bounty in its purest form, a wholesome delight in every steamed bite.

In particular, grilled mackerels taste better when grilled over briquettes. Even if you sprinkle just enough salt, grilled mackerels and white rice are like rice thieves

21. 콩국수 (Kongguksu)
: Cold Soybean Noodle Soup

Behold the ethereal Kongguksu, a chilled noodle soup that pays homage to the divine balance of simplicity and sophistication. Delicate strands of noodles waltz in a creamy broth of nutty soybeans, offering a refreshing respite from the heat of the world. With each sip, the palate is serenaded by the subtle interplay of creaminess and earthy undertones, grounded by the whisper of ground sesame seeds. Adorned with crisp cucumbers and a delicate dusting of sesame, this chilled symphony of flavors transports the senses to the very heart of Korean culinary finesse. Kongguksu isn't merely a dish; it's a testament to the artistry of transforming humble ingredients into a nourishing masterpiece, a chilled ode to subtlety that ignites the soul.

22. 멸치볶음 (Myeolchi Bokkeum)
: Stir-fried Anchovies

Myeolchi Bokkeum, the captivating Stir-fried Anchovies, dances on the palate with a symphony of savory and crispy notes. Each tiny fish, coated in a tantalizing blend of soy sauce, sugar, and sesame, transforms into a crunchy delight. The umami-packed bites, adorned with a hint of heat from red pepper flakes, create a harmonious explosion of flavors. Myeolchi Bokkeum is not merely a dish; it's a culinary escapade, an exploration of bold tastes in a compact form. These stir-fried anchovies are a testament to Korean ingenuity, turning the humble into extraordinary, and proving that small bites can carry big, delightful surprises.

23. 감자전 (Gamja Jeon)
: Potato Pancake

Gamja Jeon, the delectable Potato Pancake, is a crispy tribute to comfort and simplicity. Grated potatoes, expertly seasoned and pan-fried to golden perfection, unveil a harmonious blend of textures and flavors. Each bite is a journey through the crunchy exterior into the soft, savory core. Paired with a dipping sauce, this Korean favorite is not just a pancake; it's a celebration of the humble potato, transformed into a crispy delight. Gamja Jeon is a culinary dance of contrasts, a symphony of humble ingredients creating a dish that transcends its simplicity, proving that joy can be found in the artistry of a perfectly fried pancake.

24. 쌈 (Ssam) : Lettuce Wraps

Ssam, the art of lettuce wraps, is a culinary embrace of freshness and texture. Crispy lettuce cradles savory delights, creating a vibrant symphony in each bite. The interactive joy of assembling, dipping, and savoring transforms a meal into a shared experience. Ssam isn't just a dish; it's a celebration of balance, where greens meet bold flavors. A poetic dance of ingredients, it encapsulates the essence of communal dining, making every wrap a delightful journey through Korean culinary artistry.

25. 해물파전 (Haemul Pajeon)
: Seafood Pancake

Haemul Pajeon, a maritime masterpiece, is a crispy indulgence that echoes the sea's bounty. The medley of succulent seafood, green onions, and savory batter dances on the palate, creating a harmonious blend of textures. Each golden bite is a seaside adventure, where the ocean's essence meets the warmth of a perfectly fried pancake. Haemul Pajeon isn't just a dish; it's a celebration of coastal flavors, a delightful journey through the briny depths. With each slice, you savor the rich maritime heritage woven into the very fabric of this Korean culinary treasure.

26. 오리불고기(Duck Bulgogi)
Spicy Marinated Duck

Duck Bulgogi, a symphony of flavors, marries the richness of duck with the boldness of spicy marinade. Each succulent bite unveils a dance of sweet, savory, and spicy notes, creating a culinary masterpiece. The tender duck, bathed in the luscious marinade, offers a delightful journey for the palate. This Korean favorite isn't just a dish; it's a celebration of the exotic, a tantalizing blend of textures and tastes that elevates the dining experience. Duck Bulgogi is a captivating fusion, where the allure of duck meets the fiery spirit of Korean cuisine, leaving an indelible mark on every adventurous taste bud.

27. 빈대떡(Bindaetteok)
: Pancake with bean paste

Bindaetteok, a culinary masterpiece, intertwines the nutty richness of bean paste within a crispy golden embrace. Each bite is a dance of textures, a harmony of savory depth and delightful crunch. This Korean pancake, a celebration of tradition, encapsulates the essence of comfort and satisfaction. The earthy aroma and subtle sweetness elevate the dining experience, making each serving not just a dish but a nostalgic journey through the heart of Korean gastronomy. Bindaetteok is a symphony of flavors, where simplicity meets sophistication, leaving an indelible mark on the taste buds.

28. 쭈꾸미 볶음 (Jjukkumi Bokkeum)
: Spicy Stir-fried Baby Octopus

A spicy symphony of the sea, Stir-fried Jukkumi features tender baby jukkumi waltzing through spicy seasonings. With each bite, the flavors of the sea explode, creating an exhilarating dance in your mouth. The spiciness of the Korean spices envelops the delicate octopus, creating a harmonious blend of spice and seafood delights. This dish is not just a stir-fry, but a culinary celebration where the bounty of the sea meets the boldness of Korean cuisine. Jjukkumi Bokkeum is an adventure for the palate, an exhilarating journey through the vibrant and spicy tapestry of Korean gastronomy.

29. 호떡 (Hotteok)
: Sweet Korean Pancake

Hotteok, a sweet Korean embrace, weaves a magical spell with its golden, crispy exterior and a gooey, indulgent center. Each bite is a symphony of warmth and sweetness, an ode to the cozy delights of Korean street food. The caramelized sugar and nutty filling create a dance of flavors that transcends the ordinary pancake. Hotteok isn't just a treat; it's a nostalgic journey through the bustling streets of Korea, capturing the essence of comfort and joy in every delectable bite. It's a dessert that whispers tales of tradition and modern-day delight in perfect harmony.

30. 만두 (Mandu)
: Korean Dumplings

Mandu, Korean dumplings, are savory parcels of joy, encapsulating a symphony of flavors within delicate wrappers. Each bite is a harmonious blend of seasoned fillings—meat, vegetables, and spices—creating a culinary masterpiece. Steamed, boiled, or fried, Mandu's versatility is matched only by its ability to evoke comfort and nostalgia. These bite-sized wonders not only satisfy the palate but also tell a story of tradition and shared moments. Mandu isn't just a dumpling; it's a delectable journey through Korean culinary heritage, offering a taste of warmth, culture, and timeless delight.

Kongguksu : It is not an exaggeration to say that this is a healthy summer food for Koreans. The strong scent of beans and the taste of eating it with ice cubes and raw kimchi are hard to explain.

31. 김치볶음밥 (Kimchi Bokkeumbap)
: Kimchi Fried Rice

Kimchi Bokkeumbap, a flavor-packed journey, transforms humble ingredients into a culinary delight. The bold dance of tangy kimchi, savory rice, and a medley of spices creates a symphony on the palate. Each forkful is a spicy, comforting embrace, capturing the essence of Korean comfort food. The sizzle in the wok echoes the vibrant spirit of Korean cuisine, making Kimchi Fried Rice not just a meal but a celebration of tradition and modern flair. It's a plateful of warmth, a burst of umami, and a delicious chapter in the story of Korean gastronomy.

32. 오징어 숙회 (Ojingeo Sukhoe)
: Sliced Raw Squid Salad

Ojingeo Sukhoe, a marine delicacy, presents a delicate dance of sliced raw squid adorned in vibrant flavors. Each tender bite is a refreshing burst of oceanic essence, kissed by the subtle heat of Korean spices. The dish is a symphony of textures and tastes, where the purity of the squid meets the boldness of Korean culinary artistry. Ojingeo Sukhoe transcends the ordinary salad, offering a tantalizing journey through the briny depths, encapsulating the spirit of coastal Korea in every exquisite slice. It's a celebration of seafood, skillfully prepared to enchant the palate with its maritime charm.

33. 불닭 (Buldak)
: Spicy Fire Chicken

Buldak, the fiery thrill of Spicy Fire Chicken, is an explosive flavor journey that ignites the taste buds. The intense heat of the chili-infused marinade envelops tender chicken, creating a spicy symphony on the palate. Each fiery bite is a culinary adventure, blending the boldness of Korean spices with the succulence of perfectly cooked chicken. Buldak isn't just a spicy dish; it's a testament to the thrill-seeking spirit of Korean cuisine, where the heat is not just a sensation but an exhilarating celebration of flavor. It's a dish that sets the senses ablaze and leaves an unforgettable, spicy imprint.

34. 코다리조림 (Codari Jorim)
Braised Pollack

Codari Jorim, the indulgence of Braised Pollack, is a symphony of tender fish, soaking in a rich, savory marinade. Each bite is a harmonious blend of delicate flavors, the fish absorbing the essence of the robust sauce. The dish transcends simplicity, presenting a culinary masterpiece that reflects the artistry of Korean home cooking. With its tender, flaky texture and a dance of savory notes, Codari Jorim is not just a meal; it's a celebration of comfort, tradition, and the meticulous craft that defines Korean gastronomy. It's a dish that whispers the warmth of home in every succulent mouthful.

35. 오돌뼈 (Odolbokkeum)
: Stir-fried Spicy Pork Backbone

Odolbokkeum, the sizzling adventure of Stir-fried Spicy Pork Backbone, is a carnivore's delight. The succulent pork backbone, bathed in a fiery marinade, dances on the palate with a perfect balance of spice and umami. Each juicy bite is a journey through layers of flavor, a tantalizing blend of tender meat and bold Korean spices. Odolbokkeum transcends the ordinary, delivering a culinary spectacle that embodies the heartiness of Korean comfort food. With its robust taste and addictive heat, this dish is not just a meal; it's a celebration of bold flavors and the joy of indulging in a rich, spicy gastronomic experience.

36. 쇠고기 무국 (Sogogi Muguk)
: Beef and Radish Soup

Sogogi Muguk, the heartwarming Beef and Radish Soup, is a bowl of comfort that transcends seasons. The tender beef, paired with crisp radish, weaves a symphony of flavors in a delicate broth. Each spoonful is a journey through warmth and simplicity, a reminder of home-cooked goodness. The robust broth embraces you like a soothing embrace, making every sip a nostalgic experience. Sogogi Muguk is not just a soup; it's a timeless expression of Korean culinary love, bringing together the richness of beef, the freshness of radish, and the soul-soothing essence of homemade warmth.

37. 떡국 (Tteokguk)
: Rice Cake Soup

Tteokguk, the celebratory Rice Cake Soup, is a bowl of tradition that transcends flavors. Delicate rice cakes symbolize renewal, floating gracefully in a clear broth. Each slurp is a nod to time-honored customs, a blend of simplicity and profound meaning. Tteokguk is more than a soup; it's a cultural ritual, marking the passage of another year. The tender rice cakes represent life's continuous cycle, and the savory broth imparts the warmth of shared moments. With each spoonful, Tteokguk becomes a bridge to heritage, a reminder that in simplicity, we find the depth of tradition and the joy of new beginnings.

38. 꼬막찜 (Kkomak Jjim)
Steamed Cockles

Kkomak Jjim, the delicacy of Steamed Cockles, is a seaside symphony on the palate. Each plump cockle carries the essence of the ocean, steamed to perfection and seasoned with a melody of flavors. The briny sweetness mingles with aromatic spices, creating a dish that transports you to coastal bliss. With each succulent bite, Kkomak Jjim becomes a celebration of the sea's bounty, a harmonious dance of freshness and zest. This culinary treasure encapsulates the coastal spirit, offering a taste of the tides and a journey through the savory melodies of the ocean.

39. 부대찌개 (Budae Jjigae)
: Army Stew

Budae Jjigae, the spirited Army Stew, is a culinary experience blending history and flavor. Packed with a diverse array of ingredients, from ramen to sausages, it's a savory union born from resourcefulness. Each spoonful is a journey through time, reflecting Korea's post-war innovation and resilience. The robust broth symbolizes communal strength, making every bite a celebration of adaptation. Budae Jjigae is not just a stew; it's a testament to the fusion of tradition and ingenuity, a comforting bowl that tells a story of survival and the flavorful evolution of Korean cuisine.

40. 김치찜 (Kimchi Jjim)
: Braised Kimchi

Kimchi Jjim, the tantalizing Braised Kimchi, is a flavor symphony that unfolds on the palate. Each tender bite reveals the fermented richness of kimchi, elevated by a medley of savory spices. The slow braising process transforms the humble kimchi into a culinary masterpiece, creating a dish that is both comforting and bold. With every forkful, Kimchi Jjim is a journey through the layers of taste, a celebration of tradition, and a testament to the artistry of Korean cuisine. It's not just a dish; it's a harmonious dance of flavors that lingers, leaving a memorable imprint on the senses.

Steamed Kimchi : The combination of aged kimchi and pork is considered a heavenly combination. Rice goes in constantly.

41. 골뱅이무침 (Golbaengi Muchim)
: Spicy Sea Snail Salad

Golbaengi Muchim, the spirited Spicy Sea Snail Salad, is a culinary adventure that awakens the taste buds. Each tender sea snail, coated in a vibrant medley of spicy seasonings, delivers a symphony of flavors with each delightful crunch. The dish is a celebration of texture, marrying the chewiness of golbaengi with the boldness of spicy marinade. With every bite, golbaengi Muchim is a journey to the seaside, a lively dance of spice and freshness that captures the essence of Korean coastal gastronomy. It's not just a salad; it's a flavorful voyage that leaves a lasting impression on the palate.

42. 갓김치 (Gat Kimchi)
: Mustard Leaf Kimchi

Gat Kimchi, the zesty Mustard Leaf Kimchi, is a burst of invigorating [...] the robust mustard leaves, bathed in a piquant blend of spices, create a harmonious [...] anginess and crunch. Each bite is a journey through the bold and lively essence of [...] pickled delights. Gat Kimchi isn't just a condiment; it's a celebration of tradition, a palette of textures, and a testament to the artistry of Korean culinary craftsmanship. With its lively kick, this kimchi stands tall as a vibrant and unforgettable companion to any Korean feast.

43. 쫄면 (Jjolmyeon)
: Chewy Cold Noodles

Jjolmyeon, the delightful Chewy Cold Noodles, is a culinary adventure in every bite. Its uniquely springy texture intertwines with a symphony of flavors from the spicy and tangy sauce. The refreshing crunch of vegetables adds a delightful contrast, making each slurp a dance of contrasts. Jjolmyeon isn't just a dish; it's an experience — a refreshing, chewy escapade that invigorates the palate on a hot summer day, showcasing the playful side of Korean gastronomy.

44. 꽁치조림 (Ggongchi Jorim)
: Braised Pacific Saury

Ggongchi Jorim, the savory Braised Pacific Saury, is a symphony of oceanic flavors. The tender fish, bathed in a rich soy-based glaze, offers a delightful balance of sweet and savory notes. With each succulent bite, the essence of the sea unfolds, capturing the essence of Korean coastal cuisine. Ggongchi Jorim is not just a dish; it's a culinary ode to the maritime bounty, a celebration of simplicity and depth that resonates with every savory mouthful.

45. 닭갈비 (Dakgalbi)
: Spicy Stir-fried Chicken

Dakgalbi, the sizzling Spicy Stir-fried Chicken, is a carnival of flavors dancing on the taste buds. Tender chicken, marinated in a fiery blend of spices, char-grilled to perfection, delivers a symphony of heat and sweetness. Each vibrant bite is a journey through the lively streets of Korean cuisine, igniting the palate with an addictive combination of textures and spices. Dakgalbi isn't just a dish; it's a celebration, a culinary fiesta that encapsulates the bold spirit and zest for life found in the heart of Korean gastronomy.

46. 갈치조림 (Galchi Jorim)
: Braised Cutlassfish

Galchi Jorim, the succulent Braised Cutlassfish, beckons with a symphony of oceanic delight. This tender cutlassfish, bathed in a robust soy-based glaze, acquires savory and subtly sweet notes. Each exquisite bite encapsulates the essence of the sea, spotlighting the culinary mastery of Korean marine cuisine. More than a dish, Galchi Jorim is an odyssey into the profound flavors of the ocean—a tribute to perfectly simmered maritime treasures, leaving an unforgettable imprint on the palate and a yearning for the endless waves.

47. 열무 김치 (Yeolmu Kimchi)
: Young Radish Kimchi

Yeolmu Kimchi, the embodiment of crispness and piquancy, dances on the palate with a vibrant symphony of flavors. These young radishes, bathed in a harmonious blend of spices, deliver a delightful crunch and a burst of refreshing heat. Each bite unveils the artistry of Korean fermentation, capturing the essence of seasons in a jar. Beyond a side dish, Yeolmu Kimchi is a celebration of nature's bounty, a zesty companion that elevates any dining experience. It's a testament to Korea's culinary finesse, where simplicity and complexity converge in a jar of pickled perfection.

48. 쫄깃한 떡 (Chalgit Tteok)
: Chewy Rice Cake

Chalgit Tteok, the epitome of chewy delight, transcends the ordinary with its resilient texture. These elastic rice cakes, a harmonious blend of tradition and innovation, offer a delightful interplay of simplicity and sophistication. With each resilient bite, they weave a tale of cultural richness and culinary craftsmanship. Chalgit Tteok isn't just a treat for the palate; it's an edible art form, a testament to the ingenuity of Korean culinary traditions, providing a sensorial journey that lingers long after the last chew.

49. 우엉조림 (Ueong Jorim)
: Braised Burdock Root

Ueong Jorim, the savory Braised Burdock Root, is a tapestry of earthy flavors that transcends the ordinary. This dish, with its tender burdock root bathed in a delectable soy-based glaze, unveils a harmonious blend of natural richness and subtle sweetness. Each bite is a journey into the heart of Korean culinary artistry, where simplicity and sophistication dance in perfect unity. Ueong Jorim is not just a dish; it's a culinary ode to the art of savoring the bounties of the earth, leaving an enduring imprint of satisfaction and a yearning for the wholesome goodness of nature.

50. 북어국 (Bugeoguk)
: Dried Pollack Soup

...k, the comforting Dried Pollack Soup, is a bowl of warmth that embraces the soul. Its ...nd of dried pollack, radish, and other savory ingredients creates a harmonious sy... ...vors. With every sip, it's not just a soup; it's a sip of Korean tradition, a nourishing el... ...t transcends taste, connecting you to the soothing essence of Korean cuisine. Bugeoguk ... ...rely a dish; it's a reminder that in its simmering broth, you find a taste of home, a culinary hug that comforts and invigorates.

Can you still forget the white soup my mother made me 50 years later?

51. 깻잎장아찌 (Kkaennip Jangajji)
: Pickled Perilla Leaves

Kkaennip Jangajji, the artful dance of pickled perilla leaves, elevates the palate with a symphony of flavors. Each leaf, marinated in a medley of soy sauce, garlic, and spices, offers a harmonious blend of savory, tangy, and herbal notes. This culinary masterpiece transcends pickling, embodying the essence of Korean gastronomy. With every bite, it's not just a side dish; it's a sensorial journey, a burst of umami that captivates the taste buds and whispers the tales of tradition. Kkaennip Jangajji is more than a pickle; it's a culinary treasure, a delightful ode to the culinary heritage of Korea.

52. 콩나물국밥 (Kongnamul Gukbap)
: Bean Sprout and Rice Soup

Kongnamul Gukbap, a nourishing symphony of flavors, seamlessly blends the crisp freshness of bean sprouts with the comforting warmth of rice in a savory broth. Each spoonful is a journey through the heart of Korean culinary heritage, where simplicity meets indulgence. The delicate crunch of bean sprouts and the hearty embrace of rice create a harmonious dance on the palate, a testament to the artistry of Korean gastronomy. Kongnamul Gukbap is not just a soup; it's a celebration of wholesome ingredients, a bowlful of comfort that transcends taste, leaving a lingering melody of satisfaction.

53. 소고기 국밥 (Sogogi Gukbap)
: Beef Rice Soup

Sogogi Gukbap, the soul-soothing Beef Rice Soup, is a symphony of robust flavors and tender beef slices embraced by a hearty broth. Each spoonful unveils a harmony of comforting warmth, rich aromas, and the essence of Korean culinary tradition. The tender beef, paired with perfectly cooked rice, creates a culinary masterpiece that transcends mere sustenance. Sogogi Gukbap is not just a meal; it's a sensory journey into the heart of Korean gastronomy, leaving an indelible mark of satisfaction and a longing for its flavorful embrace.

54. 매운어묵볶음 (Maewun Eomuk Bokkeum)
: Spicy Fish Cake Stir-fry

Maewun Eomuk Bokkeum, the spirited Spicy Fish Cake Stir-fry, is a dance of fiery flavors that ignites the palate. Tender fish cakes, waltzing in a zesty sauce, create a symphony of bold and savory notes. Each bite is an exhilarating journey into the heart of Korean culinary dynamism, where the heat and depth of flavors unite in perfect harmony. This dish is not merely a culinary creation; it's a celebration of the vibrant and piquant essence that defines the soul of Korean cuisine, leaving an indelible mark on taste buds and a craving for its spirited allure.

55. 도토리묵 (Dotorimuk)
: Acorn Jelly Salad

Dotorimuk, the refreshing Acorn Jelly Salad, is a culinary symphony that captivates with its cool and delicate essence. The resilient texture of acorn jelly intertwines gracefully with a medley of crisp vegetables, creating a harmonious dance of flavors and textures. Each bite is a journey through the refreshing heart of Korean gastronomy, where simplicity meets sophistication. Dotorimuk is not merely a dish; it's a celebration of nature's bounty transformed into a delightful culinary experience, leaving an indelible mark of satisfaction and a craving for its light, wholesome goodness.

56. 꽈리고추 찜 (Kkwari Gochu Jjim) : Braised Shishito Peppers

Kkwari Gochu Jjim, the succulent Braised Shishito Peppers, dances on the palate with a tantalizing medley of flavors. These tender peppers, bathed in a savory soy-based glaze, deliver a perfect balance of mild heat and savory delight. Each bite is a journey into the heart of Korean culinary finesse, where simplicity meets a burst of nuanced tastes. Kkwari Gochu Jjim isn't just a dish; it's an edible celebration of the vibrant and diverse tastes that Korean cuisine gracefully presents, leaving an unforgettable impression of zestful satisfaction.

57. 콩자반 (Kongjaban)
: Soy Braised Soybeans

Kongjaban, the luscious Soy Braised Soybeans, unveils a dance of rich, savory flavors that linger on the palate. Each tender soybean, bathed in a delightful soy-based glaze, offers a perfect balance of sweetness and umami. This dish is a journey into the heart of Korean culinary finesse, where simplicity meets a symphony of nuanced tastes. Kongjaban is more than a dish; it's an edible poetry celebrating the humble soybean, leaving an indelible impression of wholesome satisfaction and a longing for the timeless essence of Korean gastronomy.

58. 부추전 (Buchu Jeon)
: Chive Pancake

Buchu Jeon, the delectable Chive Pancake, boasts a crisp exterior embracing a burst of freshness within. Its tantalizing blend of chives and savory batter creates a harmonious dance of flavors. With each bite, one embarks on a journey into the heart of Korean culinary finesse, where simplicity meets the intricate allure of chive-infused delight. More than a dish, Buchu Jeon is a savory ode to the vibrant essence of Korean cuisine, leaving an indelible mark of satisfaction and a yearning for its crisp, green embrace.

59. 알밥 (Albap) : Rice Bowl with Roe

Albap, the exquisite Rice Bowl with Roe, is a symphony of delicate flavors and textures. Each grain of rice cradles the essence of the sea, while the roe adds a burst of briny indulgence. The marriage of simplicity and sophistication in Korean culinary artistry is evident in every bite. Albap is not merely a dish; it's a gastronomic journey into the ocean's bounty, leaving an enduring impression of satisfaction and a yearning for the nuanced pleasures of the sea.

60. 깻잎전 (Kkaennip Jeon)
: Perilla Leaf Pancake

Kkaennip Jeon, the delectable Perilla Leaf Pancake, weaves a tapestry of vibrant flavors and crisp textures. Each bite unfolds a harmonious dance between the earthy perilla leaf and the savory batter, creating a delightful symphony on the palate. This dish epitomizes the artistry of Korean cuisine, where simplicity meets intricate layers of taste. Kkaennip Jeon isn't merely a pancake; it's a culinary poem celebrating the herbaceous richness of perilla leaves, leaving an indelible mark of satisfaction and a longing for the delightful nuances of Korean gastronomy.

Dotori Muk : It is not an exaggeration to say that it is a regular menu among Koreans' after-hiking menus.

61. 쥐포무침 (Jwipo Muchim)
: Seasoned Dried Filefish

Jwipo Muchim, the exquisite Seasoned Dried Filefish, orchestrates a symphony of flavors. In the palate, each delicate strip of filefish, seasoned to perfection, offers a dance of savory, slightly sweet, and umami notes. The subtle chewiness and marine essence encapsulate the essence of Korean culinary finesse. Jwipo Muchim is not merely a dish; it's a culinary melody celebrating the delicate transformation of dried filefish, leaving an indelible mark of satisfaction and a desire for the nuanced delights of Korean cuisine.

62. 갈치구이 (Galchi Gui)
: Grilled Cutlassfish

Galchi Gui, the enticing Grilled Cutlassfish, invites with a symphony of smoky perfection. Each bite unveils a marriage of tender flesh and charred notes, a dance of flavors that transcends the ordinary. The succulent cutlassfish, adorned with a touch of fire, embodies the artistry of Korean grilling. Galchi Gui is not merely a dish; it's a gastronomic journey into the world of grilled delights, leaving an indelible mark of satisfaction and a longing for the smoldering essence of Korean coastal cuisine.

63. 매운낙지볶음 (Maewun Nakji Bokkeum) :
Spicy Stir-fried Octopus

Maewun Nakji Bokkeum, the fiery Spicy Stir-fried Octopus, orchestrates a culinary symphony of bold heat and oceanic succulence. Each tender bite reveals the thrilling dance of spicy flavors, embracing the palate with the essence of the sea. This dish exemplifies the artistry of Korean spice mastery, where the tender octopus becomes a canvas for a spicy masterpiece. Maewun Nakji Bokkeum isn't merely a meal; it's a spicy journey into the depths of flavor, leaving an indelible mark of satisfaction and a craving for the exhilarating heat of Korean gastronomy.

64. 막국수 (Makguksu)
: Buckwheat Noodles in Cold Broth

Makguksu, the epitome of refreshing elegance, enchants with its chilled buckwheat noodles immersed in a delicate broth. Each slurp unveils a harmonious blend of earthy buckwheat and the subtle dance of savory broth, creating a cool symphony on the palate. This dish embodies the artistry of Korean culinary finesse, where simplicity and exquisite flavors intertwine. Makguksu is not just a culinary creation; it's a refreshing journey through the essence of Korean gastronomy, leaving a lasting impression of satisfaction and a craving for the cool embrace of this noodle masterpiece.

65. 깐풍기 (Kkanpunggi)
: Sweet and Spicy Garlic Fried Chicken

Kkanpunggi, the divine Sweet and Spicy Garlic Fried Chicken, is a culinary masterpiece that tantalizes the taste buds. Each crispy bite is a symphony of bold flavors, as the succulent chicken meets the perfect balance of sweetness, spiciness, and aromatic garlic. This dish embodies the artistry of Korean fried chicken, where the golden-brown exterior gives way to a burst of savory indulgence. Kkanpunggi is more than a meal; it's a flavorful journey that leaves an unforgettable impression of satisfaction and a craving for the delightful complexities of Korean gastronomy.

66. 오리양념구이 (Ori-yangnyeom-gui)
: Marinated and grilled duck with ginseng and
special sauce

Tasting duck marinated in a special sauce and roasted is a culinary adventure that goes
beyond the ordinary. The juicy duck, flavoured with our special sauce, tantalises your taste
buds with a symphony of flavours. Each bite reveals the perfect balance of flavours, creating a
memorable and enjoyable experience. This Korean delicacy not only captivates the taste buds,
but also embodies the essence of tradition and culinary art. A true masterpiece of Korean
cuisine, marinated roast duck presents a rich tapestry of flavours with a lingering aftertaste,
creating a feast to remember.

67. 닭도리탕 (Dakdoritang)
Spicy Chicken Stew

Dakdoritang, the fiery Spicy Chicken Stew, is a culinary triumph that ignites the senses. Each spoonful reveals succulent chicken, steeped in a bold and aromatic broth. The medley of spicy and savory notes creates a harmonious dance on the palate, celebrating the robust flavors of Korean cuisine. Dakdoritang isn't merely a stew; it's a flavor-packed journey into the heart of spice-laden indulgence, leaving an indelible mark of satisfaction and a yearning for the spirited warmth of this Korean culinary delight.

63 모둠전 (Modeum Jeon) - Assorted Pancakes

Modeum Jeon, the exquisite Assorted Pancakes, is a culinary symphony that dances on the taste buds. This medley of crispy and savory pancakes, each boasting its unique filling, creates a harmonious celebration of flavors and textures. From the earthy tones of kimchi jeon to the delicate silkiness of bindaetteok, every bite is a journey through the diverse landscape of Korean pancake artistry. Modeum Jeon transcends the ordinary as a gastronomic masterpiece, a delightful tapestry of tradition and innovation that leaves an indelible mark of satisfaction and a yearning for the diverse delights of Korean cuisine.

69. 순대 (Sundae)
: Korean Blood Sausage

Sundae, the savory Korean Blood Sausage, is a culinary adventure that melds bold flavors and distinctive textures. Each bite encapsulates the rich and hearty essence of the filling, harmonizing with the chewy casing. The amalgamation of earthy and robust notes creates a symphony on the palate, celebrating the complexity of Korean gastronomy. Sundae is not merely a sausage; it's a cultural delicacy, an exploration of taste that leaves an indelible mark of satisfaction and a craving for the unique and savory indulgence of this Korean culinary gem.

70. 무생채 (Musengchae)
: Shredded Radish Salad

Musengchae, the refreshing Shredded Radish Salad, is a culinary poem that dances on the palate. This dish, with its crisp radish strands, invites a symphony of textures and flavors. The subtle sweetness of the radish, combined with the zing of vinegar and the touch of sesame, creates a harmonious balance. Musengchae is a celebration of simplicity and freshness, embodying the essence of Korean culinary finesse. More than a salad, it's an ode to the vibrant and crisp delights that leave an indelible mark of satisfaction, a refreshing note in the repertoire of Korean cuisine.

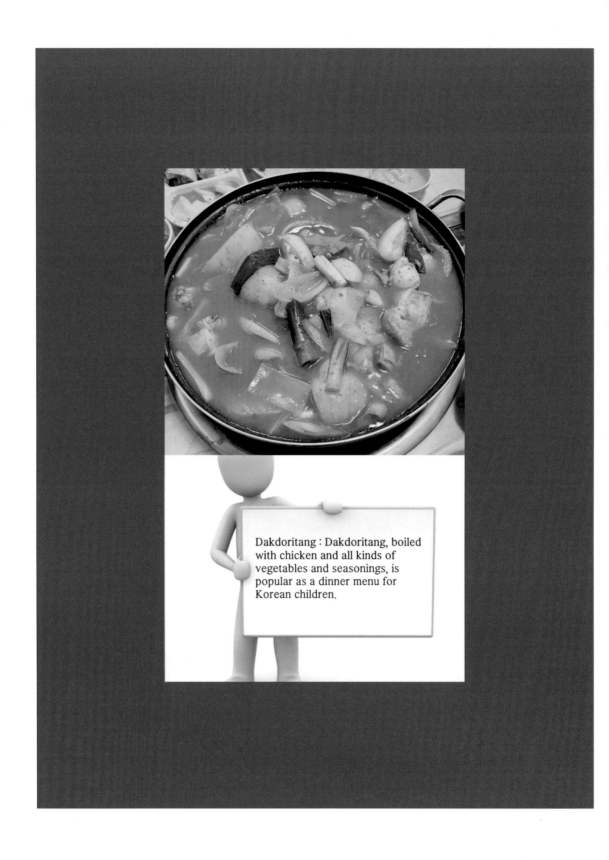

Dakdoritang : Dakdoritang, boiled with chicken and all kinds of vegetables and seasonings, is popular as a dinner menu for Korean children.

71. 소세지볶음 (Soseji Bokkeum)
: Stir-fried Sausages

Soseji Bokkeum, the savory Stir-fried Sausages, is a delightful indulgence that ignites the taste buds. Each bite offers a burst of savory flavors, as the sausages sizzle in a medley of seasonings. The caramelized exterior and juicy interior create a perfect harmony of textures. This dish is not merely a stir-fry; it's a flavorful escapade into the world of comfort cuisine, leaving an enduring impression of satisfaction and a craving for the savory notes that characterize the heart of Korean culinary joy.

72. 새우볶음밥 (Saewu Bokkeumbap)
: Shrimp Fried Rice

Saewu Bokkeumbap, the delectable Shrimp Fried Rice, is a culinary masterpiece that captures the essence of Korean gastronomy. Each grain of rice dances with succulent shrimp, creating a harmonious blend of flavors. The dish not only showcases the culinary finesse of stir-frying but also elevates the humble rice to new heights. With a medley of vegetables and the umami-rich shrimp, every mouthful is a journey into the heart of Korean comfort cuisine. Saewu Bokkeumbap isn't just a meal; it's a symphony of textures and tastes that leaves an indelible mark of satisfaction and a yearning for more.

73. 잔치국수 (Janchiguksu)
: Feast noodles

Janchiguksu, the revered Feast Noodles, is a culinary tapestry that transcends the ordinary. Delicate strands of noodles gracefully intertwine with a rich, savory broth, creating a symphony of flavors. The medley of fresh vegetables and tender meat adds a harmonious touch to this gastronomic masterpiece. Each slurp is a celebration, a journey into the heart of Korean noodle artistry that leaves an indelible mark of satisfaction and a longing for the next delightful encounter with this culinary gem.

74. 카레라이스 (Kare-rice) : Curried rice

Kare-rice, a culinary masterpiece, harmonizes aromatic Japanese curry with fluffy rice—a symphony of flavors that transcends borders. The rich, savory curry, infused with a blend of spices, caresses each grain of rice, creating a culinary canvas that is both comforting and exciting. With every bite, there's a journey through layers of warmth and spice, a delightful exploration of taste that captures the heart. Kare-rice is not just a meal; it's an odyssey of satisfaction, an invitation to savor the perfect union of Japanese culinary artistry and the simple joy of a well-cooked bowl of rice.

75. 봄동전 (Bomdong Jeon) : Wild Chive Pancake

The springtime dumpling, the delicious san dumpling, is a culinary expression of nature's bounty. With each bite, the aroma of golden brown, crisp Chinese cabbage mingles with the delicate dance of savory dough. It's a dish that embodies the artistry of Korean cuisine, combining simplicity with the vibrant flavors of wild vegetables. More than just a dish, bomdokki is a flavorful tribute to the freshness of spring, leaving an indelible mark of satisfaction and nostalgia for the seasonal pleasures that adorn the Korean table.

76. 홍어무침 (Hongeo Muchim)
: Fermented Skate Salad

Hongeo Muchim, the intriguing Fermented Skate Salad, is a bold symphony of pungent flavors that dance on the palate. The fermented skate, with its unique aroma and robust taste, is skillfully crafted into a salad that challenges and delights the senses. Each bite encapsulates the adventurous spirit of Korean gastronomy, where boldness and culinary craftsmanship converge. Hongeo Muchim is not just a dish; it's a daring exploration of fermented excellence, leaving an indelible mark of culinary curiosity and a craving for the distinctive tang of this Korean delicacy.

77. 전복죽 (Jeonbok Juk)
: Abalone Porridge

Jeonbok Juk, the exquisite Abalone Porridge, is a culinary masterpiece that whispers the essence of the sea. Each spoonful is a delicate dance of tender abalone and velvety porridge, weaving a tapestry of comforting richness. This dish embodies the harmony of simplicity and sophistication in Korean cuisine, where the ocean's treasures are transformed into a soothing, nourishing delight. Jeonbok Juk is not just a porridge; it's a culinary ode to the ocean's bounty, leaving an indelible mark of satisfaction and a yearning for the serene flavors that define Korean comfort.

78. 닭강정 (Dak Gangjeong)
: Sweet and Crispy Fried Chicken

Dak Gangjeong, the delightful Sweet and Crispy Fried Chicken, is a culinary delight that tantalizes the taste buds. Each succulent piece boasts a perfect harmony of sweetness and crispiness, creating a symphony of flavors with every bite. The golden-brown exterior encases tender chicken, showcasing the artistry of Korean fried chicken mastery. Dak Gangjeong transcends ordinary fried chicken; it's a culinary masterpiece that leaves an indelible mark of satisfaction and a longing for the delightful complexities of Korean gastronomy.

79. 깍두기 (Kkakdugi) : Cubed Radish Kimchi

Kkakdugi, the crunchy Cubed Radish Kimchi, is a flavorful journey that adds a zesty kick to any Korean meal. Each bite offers a perfect balance of spicy, sweet, and tangy notes, as the crisp radish cubes absorb the rich flavors of the kimchi seasoning. This traditional side dish is a testament to the artistry of Korean pickled delights, where the freshness of radish meets the boldness of kimchi spices. Kkakdugi is more than just a condiment; it's a burst of complexity that elevates the dining experience, leaving a memorable impression on the palate and a desire for its unique, invigorating taste.

80. 멍게 (Meongge) : Sea Pineapple

Meongge, the intriguing Sea Pineapple, is a culinary marvel that beckons with its exotic charm. Each delicate bite unveils a burst of oceanic freshness, capturing the essence of the sea in its tender, translucent flesh. The sea pineapple's subtle brininess is a testament to the treasures hidden beneath the waves. This unique marine delicacy transcends the ordinary, offering a symphony of flavors that dance on the taste buds. Meongge is not merely a seafood; it's an exploration of the sea's mysteries, leaving an indelible mark of maritime delight and a longing for the deep, blue horizons.

Abalone porridge is a health food that children and children ate when they were sick enough to be imprinted in the mind of Koreans.

81. 매운꽃게탕 (Maewun Ggotge Tang)
: Spicy Crab Soup

Maewun Ggotge Tang, the tantalizing Spicy Crab Soup, is a culinary symphony that orchestrates a dance of flavors on the palate. The succulent crab, bathed in a fiery broth, invites a thrilling medley of heat and oceanic richness. Each spoonful is a journey into the heart of Korean gastronomy, where the bold spice and delicate crab meat harmonize in a delightful duet. Maewun Ggotge Tang isn't merely a soup; it's a spicy ode to the sea's bounty, leaving an indelible mark of satisfaction and a yearning for the invigorating warmth of Korean culinary artistry.

82. 생선전 (Saengseon Jeon)
: Pan-fried Fish

Saengseon Jeon, the delectable Pan-fried Fish, is a culinary marvel that captures the essence of the sea in every golden bite. The tender fish, coated in a light batter, achieves a perfect balance of crispiness and succulence. Each piece is a journey through the delicate art of Korean pan-frying, where simplicity accentuates the natural flavors. Saengseon Jeon is not just a dish; it's a celebration of maritime delights, leaving an indelible mark of satisfaction and a longing for the crisp, golden perfection of Korean seafood cuisine.

83. 삼계탕 (Samgyetang)
: Ginseng Chicken Soup

Samgyetang, the nourishing Ginseng Chicken Soup, is a sublime elixir that harmonizes health and indulgence. Each spoonful unveils a symphony of flavors, as tender chicken, fragrant ginseng, and delicate herbs dance in a broth of pure goodness. This Korean culinary gem not only satiates the palate but also rejuvenates the spirit. Samgyetang is more than a soup; it's a comforting embrace, a celebration of vitality and tradition, leaving an enduring imprint of satisfaction and a yearning for the wholesome warmth of Korean gastronomy.

84. 동태찌개 (Dongtae Jjigae)
: Pollack Stew

Dongtae Jjigae, the heartwarming Pollack Stew, is a comforting melody of oceanic richness.
The tender pollack, nestled in a broth of savory perfection, releases a symphony of flavors
that capture the essence of the sea. Each spoonful is a journey into the soul-soothing warmth
of Korean cuisine, where the purity of ingredients harmonizes to create a culinary
masterpiece. Dongtae Jjigae transcends mere sustenance; it's an ode to the maritime treasures,
leaving an indelible mark of satisfaction and a longing for the comforting embrace of this
Korean culinary classic.

85. 새우튀김 (Saewu Twigim)
: Tempura Shrimp

Saewu Twigim, the delightful Tempura Shrimp, is a crispy revelation that tantalizes the taste buds with a perfect union of succulence and crunch. Each golden-coated shrimp encapsulates a symphony of flavors, showcasing the artistry of deep-frying mastery in Korean cuisine. The delicate balance of textures, from the shatteringly crisp exterior to the juicy, tender shrimp within, is a testament to culinary finesse. Saewu Twigim is not just a dish; it's a culinary spectacle that leaves an indelible impression of satisfaction, inviting one to savor the harmonious marriage of flavor and texture in every glorious bite.

86. 문어숙회 (Muneo Sukhoe)
: Steamed Octopus Salad

Muneo Sukhoe, the exquisite Steamed Octopus Salad, is a culinary poetry that unfolds with each delicate bite. The tender octopus, artfully steamed to perfection, presents a marriage of oceanic freshness and subtle sweetness. Complemented by a symphony of crisp vegetables and nuanced dressing, each mouthful is a journey into the refined elegance of Korean seafood cuisine. Muneo Sukhoe transcends the ordinary; it's a flavorful ballet of textures and tastes that leaves an indelible mark of satisfaction, inviting one to relish the harmony of flavors in this enchanting Korean culinary creation.

87. 돼지국밥 (Dwaeji Gukbap)
: Pork and Rice Soup

Dwaeji Gukbap, the comforting Pork and Rice Soup, is a gastronomic embrace that warms both the body and soul. Each spoonful unveils the tender pork, delicately seasoned and mingling with perfectly cooked rice in a hearty broth. This Korean culinary gem embodies the art of balance, where savory richness meets the simplicity of grains. Dwaeji Gukbap is more than a soup; it's a harmonious symphony of flavors, leaving an indelible mark of satisfaction and a desire for the soothing warmth of this traditional Korean dish.

88. 돼지불고기 (Dwaeji Bulgogi)
: Spicy Marinated Pork

Dwaeji Bulgogi, the fiery Spicy Marinated Pork, captivates the palate with a tantalizing blend of bold flavors. Each succulent piece of pork, bathed in a spicy marinade, offers a perfect harmony of heat, sweetness, and savory delight. This Korean culinary masterpiece showcases the art of marination, where tender pork becomes a canvas for a symphony of tastes. Dwaeji Bulgogi isn't just a dish; it's a flavorful journey into the heart of Korean spice, leaving an indelible mark of satisfaction and a longing for the vibrant notes of this spicy delicacy.

89. 꼼장어볶음 (kkomjangeo-bokkeum)
Stir-fried spicy eel

Kkomjangeo-bokkeum, the delectable stir-fried spicy eel, is a culinary crescendo of flavors. The tender eel, bathed in a fiery glaze, dances on the palate with a perfect harmony of heat and sweetness. Each succulent bite is a journey into the heart of Korean gastronomy, where the richness of eel is elevated by a symphony of spices. Kkomjangeo-bokkeum isn't just a dish; it's a spicy serenade, leaving an indelible mark of satisfaction and a craving for the bold, nuanced notes of Korean culinary excellence.

90. 추어탕 (Chueotang) : Loach soup

Chueotang, the savory loach soup, is a soothing elixir that captures the essence of Korean comfort. The delicate broth, infused with loach and fragrant herbs, unfolds a symphony of flavors—subtle, yet profound. Each spoonful is a journey into the heart of traditional Korean nourishment, where simplicity and depth intertwine. Chueotang isn't merely a soup; it's a warm embrace, leaving an indelible mark of satisfaction and a yearning for the gentle comforts of Korean culinary heritage.

Pork and rice soup: It is a representative menu of common people's food that Koreans can eat anytime, anywhere in the four seasons.

91. 대구찜 (Daegujjim) : Steamed codfish

A culinary masterpiece that will elevate your meal to the next level. Delicately steamed, tender cod is a symphony of flavors that captures the essence of Korean cuisine. Each bite is a journey into a gourmet world where simplicity meets unparalleled flavor. Steamed cod is a culinary tribute to the bounty of the sea that transcends the ordinary, leaving an indelible mark of satisfaction and nostalgia for the delicate pleasures of Korean maritime cuisine.

92 조개구이 (Jogae-gui) : Grilled clam

A culinary masterpiece that will elevate your meal to the next level. Delicately steamed, tender cod is a symphony of flavors that captures the essence of Korean cuisine. Each bite is a journey into a gourmet world where simplicity meets unparalleled flavor. Steamed cod is a culinary tribute to the bounty of the sea that transcends the ordinary, leaving an indelible mark of satisfaction and nostalgia for the delicate pleasures of Korean maritime cuisine.

93. 대게찜 (Daegejjim) : steamed king crab

Daegejjim, the regal steamed king crab, reigns as a majestic delight in Korean culinary culture. Each succulent leg, bathed in a fragrant steam, unveils the unrivaled sweetness of the sea. The tender, flaky crab meat, kissed by steam's embrace, showcases the pinnacle of oceanic indulgence. Daegejjim is not just a dish; it's a royal feast that crowns the taste buds with the rich, buttery essence of the king crab, leaving an enduring mark of satisfaction and a yearning for the opulent flavors of the deep.

94. 선짓국 (Seonjitguk)
: Hangover soup with ox-blood

Seonjitguk, the comforting Hangover Soup with ox blood, is a remedy that transcends the boundaries of culinary medicine. This revitalizing broth, enriched with the robust essence of ox blood, serves as a balm for the weary soul. Each sip is a journey into the heart of Korean gastronomy, where the melding of flavors becomes a healing elixir. Seonjitguk is not merely a soup; it's a testament to the curative powers of tradition and taste, leaving an indelible mark of rejuvenation and a longing for the comforting embrace of this unique remedy.

95. 가오리찜 (Gaorijim) : Steamed raw ray fish

Gaorijim, the delicacy of steamed raw ray fish, is a culinary marvel that elevates the palate to new heights. This ethereal dish, with its tender and succulent ray fish, embodies the artistry of Korean seafood cuisine. The subtle flavors, brought to life through the steaming process, create a symphony of taste that resonates with the essence of the sea. Gaorijim is not just a meal: it's a gastronomic journey into the purity of raw seafood, leaving an indelible mark of delight and a yearning for the sublime pleasures of Korean maritime delicacies.

96. 굴전 (Guljeon) : Pan-fried oysters

Guljeon, the epitome of pan-fried oysters, is a culinary masterpiece that captivates the senses. Each bite unfolds a symphony of textures, from the crisp outer layer to the succulent, briny core. This dish embodies the essence of Korean seafood artistry, where the richness of oysters meets the skillful finesse of pan-frying. Guljeon is not merely a meal; it's a sensory journey into the ocean's bounty, leaving an indelible impression of satisfaction and a lingering desire for the delectable flavors of Korean maritime delights.

97. 간장게장 (Ganjang-gejang)
: Crab marinated in soy sauce

Ganjang-gejang, the sublime soy sauce-marinated crab, is a culinary delight that harmonizes the ocean's richness with the depth of soy essence. Each meticulously marinated crab carries a symphony of savory, sweet, and briny notes, creating an exquisite dance of flavors on the palate. This dish represents the pinnacle of Korean seafood craftsmanship, where the succulence of crab meets the nuanced art of soy-based perfection. Ganjang-gejang is not just a culinary experience; it's a gastronomic journey into the heart of meticulous preparation, leaving an enduring imprint of satisfaction and a craving for the refined indulgence of Korean seafood cuisine.

98. 곰탕 (Gomtang) : Boiled bone stew

Gomtang, the comforting boiled bone stew, is a culinary embrace that transcends simplicity. This nourishing broth, crafted from slow-simmered bones, whispers tales of tradition and warmth. Each spoonful unveils a delicate dance of flavors, where the richness of beef melds seamlessly with the subtle whispers of garlic and green onions. Gomtang is a testament to the artistry of Korean comfort cuisine, offering a soothing journey into the heart of hearty, soul-nurturing goodness. It's not just a stew; it's a bowl of comfort, leaving an indelible mark of satisfaction and a yearning for the timeless warmth of Korean culinary heritage.

99. 다슬기국 (Daseulgitguk)
: Small freshwater snail soup

Daseulgitguk, the delicate small freshwater snail soup, is a culinary journey into the subtle wonders of Korean flavors. Each sip tells a tale of pristine broths, where the essence of small freshwater snails intertwines with gentle whispers of herbs and roots. The result is a harmonious blend that transcends simplicity, offering a taste that is both comforting and unique. Daseulgitguk is not just a soup; it's a poetic celebration of the untamed delights that nature provides, leaving an enduring impression of satisfaction and a longing for the nuanced pleasures of Korean gastronomy.

100. 대구탕 (Daegutang) : Cod soup

Daegutang, or cod soup, is a sublime harmony of delicate flavors, embodying the essence of Korean culinary finesse. The broth, enriched with the robustness of cod, whispers tales of the sea, while the medley of vegetables adds a symphony of textures. With each spoonful, there's a dance of umami, a comforting warmth that resonates. Daegutang is not just a dish; it's an oceanic embrace, a celebration of simplicity and sophistication in every spoonful, leaving a lingering, savory memory that beckons you back to the seaside essence of Korean gastronomy.

Steamed stingray : It's a precious dish that can be eaten mainly near Korean ports. A fantastic combination of seasoning and stingray. Oh, I'm craving it so much.

"The Korean Kitchen: A Visual Feast of 100 Authentic Flavors"

발 행 | 2024년 01월 18일
저 자 | 리차드홍
펴낸이 | 한건희
펴낸곳 | 주식회사 부크크
출판사등록 | 2014.07.15(제2014-16호)
주 소 | 서울특별시 금천구 가산디지털1로 119 SK트윈타워 A동 305호
전 화 | 1670-8316
이메일 | info@bookk.co.kr

ISBN | 979-11-410-6762-5

www.bookk.co.kr